WHAT BOOKS PRESS

AN IMPRINT OF

THE GLASS TABLE

COLLECTIVE

LOS ANGELES

DREAMER PARADISE

DREAMER PARADISE

DAVID QUIROZ

WHAT BOOKS PRESS

LOS ANGELES

Library of Congress Cataloging-in-Publication Data

Names: Quiroz, David, author.
Title: Dreamer paradise / David Quiroz.
Other titles: Dreamer paradise (Compilation)
Description: Los Angeles : What Books Press, 2024. | Summary: "To be
    undocumented, to be America's shadow, can be the worst thing any youth
    or adolescent can experience. In some cases, undocumented immigrant
    youth will only learn that they are undocumented once it is time to
    apply for jobs, a driver's license, or college applications because to
    apply requires a valid social security number. The term 'Dreamer' is now
    claimed by the undocumented youth population. It redefines the
    experience of immigrant youth and validates their existence as an
    individual experience. Dreamer Paradise aims to tell that experience and
    serves as a closer look into Quiroz's life, from being denied entry at
    the DMV to wanting acceptance as an American citizen; and, at the same
    time, holding their Mexican queer identity close to their existence.
    Quiroz does not hold back and urges anyone who reads to listen"--
    Provided by publisher.
Identifiers: LCCN 2024018822 | ISBN 9798990014909 (trade paperback)
Subjects: LCGFT: Poetry.
Classification: LCC PS3617.U595 D74 2024 | DDC 811/.6--dc23/eng/20240509
LC record available at https://lccn.loc.gov/2024018822

Cover art: Gronk, *Untitled*, mixed media on paper, 2023
Book design by ash good, www.ashgood.com

What Books Press
363 South Topanga Canyon Boulevard
Topanga, CA 90290

WHATBOOKSPRESS.COM

Para mi mamá,
mi papá,
Carlos, Kathee, Arlo,
y Alan

Para Marvin from EOP,
Arlena Tupaz,
The Boys and Girls Club of San Fernado Valley,
y para el Centro de Aprendizaje Vaughn Next Century,
San Fernando Ca.

LEAVES FROM THE VINE

—After *Avatar the Last Airbender*, "Tales of Ba Sing Se"

Leaves from the vine
Falling so slow
Like fragile tiny shells
Drifting in the foam

Little *DACA* boy
Come marching home

Brave *DACA* boy
Comes marching

home

"No matter how simple it might appear at first glance, every translation is thick with linguistic choices that carry political and aesthetic implications. Some of these choices—like leaving certain culturally specific terms in the language of the original—are immediately visible; Some others are not. Certain terms, for example, demand to be left in their original form. These are often described as "untranslatables."

—*Witches,* Brenda Lozano

DACA

noun

/da ka/ • Deferred Action for Childhood Arrivals

1. ~~American~~
2. Human / ~~Person~~
3. ~~Not an~~ illegal alien

DACA DACA DACA DACA DACA DACA DACA DACA DACA DACA DACA DACA
DACA DACA DACA DACA DACA DACA DACA DACA DACA DACA DACA DACA

DACA DACA DACA DACA DACA DACA DACA DACA DACA DACA DACA DACA
DACA DACA DACA DACA DACA DACA DACA DACA DACA DACA DACA DACA

DACA DACA DACA DACA DACA DACA DACA DACA DACA DACA DACA DACA
DACA DACA DACA DACA DACA DACA DACA DACA DACA DACA DACA DACA

DACA DACA DACA DACA DACA DACA DACA DACA DACA DACA DACA DACA
DACA DACA DACA DACA DACA DACA DACA DACA DACA DACA DACA DACA

DACA DACA DACA DACA DACA DACA DACA DACA DACA DACA DACA DACA
DACA DACA DACA DACA DACA DACA DACA DACA DACA DACA DACA DACA

DACA DACA DACA DACA DACA DACA DACA DACA DACA DACA DACA DACA
DACA DACA DACA DACA DACA DACA DACA DACA DACA DACA DACA DACA

"Sometimes called Dreamers"—Obama, *2012*

INSIDE

ONE, ILLEGAL

TWO, DREAMER LOVE

~~ILLEGAL~~

DREAMER PARADISE

The crows sing the ballads of my heart.
They sing my songs, and I am left alone on
this road.

+

Rocky,
filled with tiny pebbles that get stuck
underneath my shoes.

My American shoes.

I can hear the crows from a distance as I
continue to walk this path of rocks.

+

Up beyond,
I see the windows and the reflection of this
country looking right back.

I see without seeing.
I feel without feeling.
I breathe without breathing.

I see the light that shines on everything
except *me*.
I see the first and the last of me.

+

Here,
I kneel in mercy,
asking for a different reflection. To stop

dreaming because dreams are false
prophecies.

+

Dreams get me in trouble.
Dreams push me away into the darkness,
into the cold, and I am left mute.

+

Freedom is accepting consequences.

+

I need a voice.
I need my voice.
There's nothing left but these pebbles.
No more rain. There's only

+

paradise.
I am not broken.
I am not tired.
I am not lonely.
    I am here.

+

It is green. Some yellow. Some orange.
   No gray in sight.

It is soothing to hear the critters.
They tell each other secrets.
They tell each other love stories as they hide
from the bigger animals.

+

I am the bigger animal.
I am the wolf who howls under the stars.
I am the tiny bird looking for its nest.
I am the trail and the footprints.
I am the mountains.
I am the lake.
I am the dreamer.

I   am   a   *Dreamer*

TUXPAN, MICHOACÁN

Even my road
has roads.

In the open,

I see
the aloe that soothes my skin turn to dust.

The sun's rays invade my dreams and call them
unholy.

Erase me. ~~Remember~~ me. Erase me.

past. present. future.

This path doesn't care to remember me.

I am looking for a reason to write this poem and
a dream. I am left without dreaming. I have no
more dreams, butterflies, flowers, water, or air.

I can't go back.

580,000 Americans

580,000 Americans and I am one of them.

I misplaced my footprints on this arduous way.

+ Wear our mother's and father's skin.
+ Wear our work gear and uniforms.
+ Wear our part-time shoes.
+ Wear work masks and assemble.

| holding | is the | health | we have. |
| hands. | only. | care. | |

We pay our dues.

[Punch in | ~~Punch out~~ Unavailable]

$$+$$

The hands of my ancestors guide me. They hold me tightly. They hold me.

I believe in a world that looks at me and thinks of me.

One day, America will think of *me*.

I am dreaming

again.

580,000

There once was a hungry eagle looking for food.
After some hours, it spotted a rabbit.
For the eagle, this was no easy catch.
Rabbits are swift jumpers and seekers and camouflage well with Mother Earth.

The eagle swayed from the tallest tree in the valley and captured the tiny rabbit with a single puncture to the heart.

A trickster fox nearby carefully awaited the eagle to capture the rabbit.
The fox was also hungry, but with no virtue or mercy for the eagle's catch, the fox stole half of the rabbit when the eagle was not looking.

The greedy fox laughed at the eagle, "HA. HA. HA."

When the eagle noticed half of its dinner missing, he grew confused.
Who would steal from the eagle?
The eagle planned to use the remaining of its food as bait because *nobody* stole from the king of the sky.

Unaware of the trap, and the desire for more food, the greedy fox returned to steal the other half of the rabbit.

As the fox pranced away with the other half, claiming victory, the eagle snatched the thief.
The fox pleaded with the eagle.
He asked for forgiveness.

He cried.
And cried.
And cried.

The eagle was poisoned with hate.
The thorns of victory punctured the fox.

| because | from the | of | sky. |
| nobody stole | king | the | |

+ +

"When Mother Nature sends its foxes to our valley, they're not sending their best. They're sending the foxes that have lots of problems, and they're bringing those problems to us. They're bringing drugs. They're bringing crime. They're rapists of our valley."

Whistled the eagle for *all* to hear.

I struggle with choosing an identity.
Who does my country want me to be?

am I the eagle,
the fox,
or the rabbit?

HERE TO STAY

To the confused,
seekers of truth,
to those holding the signs,
"Go Back to Your Country!"
what is your fear?

It has many faces and knows
many dreams, the reclamation of
 my

        liberty,
        happiness,
        and justice.

My justice

To be powerful in my DACA-loving self,
an added political connotation.

My DACA
An encapsulation of my politics.

My flags

I
am

                home.

AMERICAN

When I check el refri for food, and all I find are brown frijoles and a tiny piece of queso fresco.

When I answer the phone and say, "bueno!" instead of hello.

When my mom sends me to the Carniceria on the corner of Herrick Avenue to buy long-distance phone cards.

> *But make sure to buy the card that sings the love ballads of your mother's first love, Los Temerarios, exposing your mother's secrets, $ 5.00 a card.*

Cuando el hijo de puta (el jefe) no quiere pagar.

When I needed school supplies, but we also needed packs of tortillas and tiny bags of sopas de fideo.

When we stood in line at local churches for expired food, Daisy from class was standing there too—

    [cheeks like cherry].

When my mom showed up at the parent conference, I mixed and matched my two tongues

    right in front of my teacher.

MERETRICIOUS

*

I felt traffic in my head
and the exhaustion of his
fingers like he'd been laying brick
for eight hours straight,
which he was.

I didn't ask for this,
a melody I had made up
in my head

     was
playing
        and
   playing
        on
repeat.

* *

While my friends were
getting in line at the DMV,
excited for driver's permits and
identifications,

I was told:
   + Appointments
   + Non-appointments
   + Americans

only.

* * * *

I felt like a hummingbird without
sweet water.

Like flowers do in California
summers
after
¿Por qué necesitas la matrícula
consular?
each
¿A qué edad llegó a los Estados
Unidos?
question.

* * * * *

The official reached out from
his tiny box and handed me the
receipt with my newly printed
"government" ID.

With the Mexican seal glossing
across the meretricious card.

✳ ✳ ✳

I felt embarrassed at the
Mexican Consulate sometime
before graduating in 2011.

I made an appointment to
see a Mexican official.

Spanish Only for all
appointments.

I tried my best to decipher the
puzzle of words on the
application, but the sentences
laughed at me instead.

The way people laugh after a
bad joke.
Years of speaking
Spanglish instead of
proper jargon
was the real joke.

* * * * * *

I felt traffic in my head and
returned to work
with my dad.

He picked
me up on 6th Street.

He was playing K-Love radio.

I didn't ask for this
on repeat.

TEARS

I surrender my voice for submission.

I open my vault and unleash my oath
to prove I *am* an American citizen
just like you.

I surrender my politics and ask you
to encapsulate my loyalty on a
government-issued identity.

My government.

I surrender my Mexico

I surrender my Spanish

I surrender my
        maíz
        frijoles
        nopales

Don't mistake my poetry for tears.
I am not broken.

Don't mistake my poetry and call me ungrateful.

I've earned
my
seat
at
the
table.

PROMISES WALK

As if this American flag looking at me ain't enough,
I have tears of freedom pouring on me from
too much laughter.

When will my *America* be enough?

How do you feel being so perfect but not perfect enough?

We were promised a paradise, but that promise will
always walk the plank.

It's a crow dressed as a hummingbird.

It's a lie dancing at the masquerade ball.

aka

DACA

SELF MY

Freedom has me in chains.

I do not eat.
I do not sleep.
I do not think.

For me

My
+
Self

Freedom carries me everywhere she goes;
she doesn't trust me.

She won't take her eyes off of me.

I don't see the sun.
I don't feel love.
I can't touch kindness.
I can't feel my own heartbeat.
I can't find my own shadow,
where's my shadow?

The white man said it was free, so I took it.
Now, I'm paying for it with interest.

There are degrees of free.

I fear. No matter. How _____ (much, little, less, more) I love.
America.

She will never love me back.

THE LATTER

This country is confused about
its own
$$|i\,d\,e\,n\,|\,t\,i\,t\,y\,|;$$

how dare it ask for mine

The weight of my last name,
my version of English,
my version of Spanish.

To be lost in a maze of conflicting

_____.

dreams/stories/dualities

To live on the border.

It scares you. It scares me.

$$+\ +\ +$$

It be in my face, *my* America

    01. Renew my work permit or
            forfeit my career
    02. Renew my work permit or
            forfeit my brand new car
    03. Renew my work permit or
            forfeit my mortgage
    04. Renew my work permit or
            forfeit *me*

America,

You don't want me in the middle.

By choosing one side, I surrender the other.
By choosing no side, I surrender _____.

This country always picks sides.
Never my side.
Not since my first pledge of allegiance.

    01. Dreamer, go back to "my" country.
    02. Dreamer, stay in "my" country.

I'm on the latter.

RUMOR

If rumors and dreams stitched my
land together,

what's the rumor about me?

I'm the worst rumor.

I have no numbers.

> *No last name*
> *No America*
> *No border*

No words left for this poem.

All I have is this journey.

And a rumor.

> *No voice*
> *No tomorrow*
> *No stars*

Abandoned.

As if this journey was born from
my

                          rumors.

MARIBEL

and I sat next to each other on our way to UCLA on our sophomore year
"College is for Everyone" field trip.

I met Maribel on a vague occasion in 7th grade. * What do you say to someone you've only spoken to a handful of times but feel like you've known forever? It was awkward sitting next to a familiar stranger.

We were both twelve and wore the same school uniforms. She walked with the popular girl at school, and I always wondered how they became friends. How does someone like Maribel, the * most intelligent girl in school, become friends with the prettiest girl?

I broke the silence and asked about her upcoming Quince.

*

*   *   *   *   *   *

At home, she disappointed her mom the most.   *   I asked her about her damas and chambelanes, the dance court for her party.

If her mom could ask her one question: Do you like boys or girls?

She said she was missing one.

*

She was in the honors program, a gifted reader, and a math extraordinaire

At the end of the trip, we exchanged numbers. Some days later, she called and asked if I wanted to join her court.

Nothing was wrong with her.   *

—was it weird that I said yes?—

Her pride flag was hidden behind her spiffy glasses—I didn't know it then, but my gaydar has improved.

ii.

When Maribel left for UCSD, we saw the Google Maps automobile cruising the 818 projects.

If you Google: *Why is there a Google Maps car?* **Google will respond:** To match each image to its geographic location on the map.

If you Google: "Pacoima Projects," you'll notice building 68 needs an updated image.

If Google Maps prioritized brown communities, the world would see how many things have changed.

It was the first time we had seen the Google Maps Car. The little shuttle was exiting unit 415.

Do you think she'll come back soon?

iii.
We were both sixteen and looking for
part-time jobs anywhere and
everywhere.

It was easy for Maribel to apply for
jobs [she had a ~~social security~~
~~number~~].

Breaking News on Univision:

One day, after school, I asked for something embarrassing.
On the corner of Van Nuys Blvd and Pacoima is a man
selling fake socials and Tarjetas de Residencia. We went on
Monday, but the man wasn't there. Another man told us to
come back on a Wednesday. On Wednesday, we discovered
the man no longer had a business.

Drive-by Shooting in Pacoima

I never had the   I hugged my
chance to apply   dearest friend
for jobs at sixteen.   from The
                         Pacoima Projects.
                                                   ~~Salvation~~

In |solidarity|,   I hated her for
Maribel didn't   leaving me, but   ~~Freedom~~ bible
either.   higher education
                         would be her

                                                  who knows what
                                                   she would see
                                                    before me?

24

BARGAIN

I met a bargainer at the corner of
Cornelius Street at the stop sign.

He held his left hand, suggesting I
help him cross over to me.

I denied him several times.
"I don't talk to strangers!"
I yelled and yelled.

He held a long list of names and
numbers with his right hand. He
was the dream bargainer.

He bargains dreams. Makes them
come true. Small fee applies.

He asked for my hand in marriage.

How could I deny my future?

*June 15, 2012 – President Obama Signs Deferred Action for Childhood
Arrivals (DACA) to Allow Some Undocumented Immigrants Who Came
to the United States as Children to Stay in the Country.*

I signed away my life to a part-time job.

Full time.

The fine print explained it all, but who reads the fine print?

Not a dreamer like me.

We were marked with numbers, and every two years, the bargainer would decide,

are you a dreamer worth bargaining with?

I-821D SCREENING

Please tell the truth, or your application can be denied

----

1   Were you under 31 as of   [*] Yes [ ]No
    June 15, 2012, when the DACA program
    was first announced?

2   Did you enter the United States before   [*] Yes [ ]No
    turning 16?

3   Have you continuously lived in   [*] Yes [ ]No
    The United States, since June 15, 2007,
    up to the present?

4   Were you physically present in The   [*] Yes [ ]No
    United States on June 15, 2012,
    and when requesting DACA?—*Can you prove it?—*

5   Are currently enrolled in school,   [*] Yes [ ]No
    have graduated from high school,
    or have obtained a certificate of
    completion?

6   Have you been convicted   [ ] Yes [*]No
    of a felony or significant
    misdemeanor offense?

7   Are you a threat to national security or public safety?   [ ] Yes [*]No

On your next appointment,
I need evidence that supports
your claims, along with a
money order or personal
check for $465.00 made out
to the Department of Homeland
Security.

LLORONA

no longer weeps for her children, for why forlorn
hope?

This desert is filled with rotten bodies and
trapped souls that have latched themselves to
broken toys.

One toy at a time, she cleans the desert.
She fills a black bag:
    01. Power Ranger de Omar
    02. Muñeca de Olivia
    03. Patito de Pedro

On record, they're classified as items:
    01. evidence one
    02. evidence two
    03. evidence three

The bus ride home was long, and my mom's
worried face was uttering a thousand words
without a word
in her mouth.

To say she was uneasy would be belittlement.

I was to submit my life, to condense the essence
of who I am on paper.

To prove my love for this country, as if pledging
allegiance in first grade, second grade, or fifth
grade wasn't enough.

Who was going to pay for my
Dream Deferred?

Llorona, can I borrow $465.00 and a black bag?

CULT

I pledge allegiance to *my DACA*

and to the *strict rules*

for which it stands,

one *renewal,*

every two years,

with *a $495 fee*

and *probational freedom*

for all *that*

qualify.

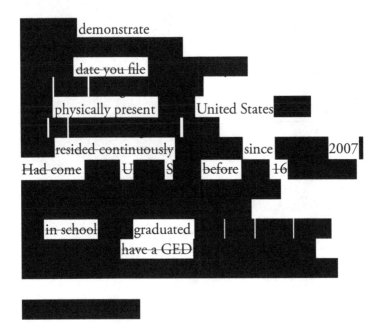

demonstrate

date you file

physically present   United States

resided continuously   since   2007

Had come   U   S   before   16

in school   graduated

have a GED

—USCIS.GOV/DACA

CHAINS

you have to believe in it blindly

you cannot ask questions

because they deny you

entry

we have no other god, we only believe in

DACA

one god

DACA

one deity

DACA

one dream

DACA

           it is religious and political freedom

           I call it

           chains

           on chains

           on chains

DREAMER LOVE

LOVE LETTER

It is a love letter to *me* when you call me a
dreamer.

When I check off boxes (or don't),
apply for jobs,
for free money,
apply at life.

I am reminded of my power:
+ my forcefield
+ my shield
+ my badge of honor

when you call me,
              soñador

        It is a love letter to my mom.
        when they call her son a dreamer.

        She'd make limonada for Carlos and me. Alan
        wasn't born yet. It was our religion to sit under
        the Pepper tree and do our homework together.
        Our religion to dream together.

        She didn't speak a word in e n g l i s h, but she
        was always there, helping me dream.

It is a love letter to my dad when they call his gay
boy a dreamer.

A day laborer with a hundred jobs, and always a
100 short on rent.

A skilled man con pocas oportunidades.

BOXES

My friend Daniela likes to say,
"You're a walking hate crime
waiting to happen."

ill	g	b
eg	a	r
al	y	o
		w
		n
☐	☐	☐

She forgot

ed	grad	ba
uc	uate	da
at		ss
ed		
☐	☐	☐

NOVEMBER 9, 2016

Swollen eyes
with heavy pockets

                held back tears
                from the night before.

Is this real?
I rub my eyes in disbelief
Now what?

                I brushed my teeth
                and rolled my deodorant,
                leaving the white residue
                behind.

I changed into slacks
and combed my hair

                like *normal.*

I declare, today,
a regular day.

                Until Luis asked
                from his desk:
          —he raised his
          hand this time—

Mr.
you know how
Trump
      won?

            —yes—

Will my parents be

                deported?

        —I don't know.—

TRUE OR FALSE

		T	F
1	"Anyone can apply for DACA"	☐	☐
2	"This program will entice criminals to come to America"	☐	☐
3	"It is a pathway to citizenship"	☐	☐
4	"It is a free program that hard-working Americans pay for"	☐	☐
5	DACA recipients "put our nation at risk of crime, violence, and terrorism"	☐	☐
6	"DACA recipients do not pay taxes"	☐	☐
7	"You must reveal your DACA status to anyone when asked"	☐	☐
8	"DACA people are not real Americans"	☐	☐
9	"Only Mexicans are DACA"	☐	☐
10	"Over 75 percent of American citizens are in favor of DACA and favor a permanent solution to the immigrant crisis"	☐	☐

statements. mentioned. above. are statements. I have heard people say in open conversation. on the news. commentators (professionals). anti DACA folk.

in front of me | kcab ym dniheb.

1 [F], 2 [F], 3 [F], 4 [F], 5 [F], 6 [F], 7 [F], 8 [F], 9 [F], 10 [T]

EAVESDROPPING

I overheard
a woman
talking

Her two sons are
DACA recipients

"Ellos son DACA"

She'd tell everyone

How do I tell her
not to tell strangers
her son's deepest
secrets?

ÚLTIMA HORA @ WORK

9:05 a.m.
I don't check my
phone at work.

9:10	**NPR Alert**	"Trump Ends DACA, Calls on Congress To Act"
9:12	**iMessage Carlos**	"YO WTF."
9:16	**Missed Call** **Mom*heart emoji***	
9:17	**Voicemail** **Mom*heart emoji***	"Te quiero, no te preocupes."
9:18	**Text message from** **Mom*heart emoji***	
New	**Twitter [View | Close]**	
New	**Twitter [View | Close]**	
New	**Twitter [View | Close]**	
New	**Twitter [View | Close]**	
New	**CNN [View | Close]**	
New	*go*	
New	*home*	
New	*dreamer*	
New	*!*	
Now	**GMAIL [View | Close]**	United We Dream: "Home is Here"

I don't check my
phone at work.

HEADLINES

Llorona sways through
the Sonoran Desert,
guarding dreamers that
seek impossible dreams.

Dec 26, 2018   'Dreamers' and Trump's dream of a wall

Jan 10, 2018   Take a deal for the dreamers. Build the wall.

Jan 19, 2019   Trump offers protection for 'dreamers' in exchange for
the border.

Jan 2, 2019   Cut a deal, build Trump's wall, and protect Dreamers.

Mar 19, 2018   Border wall Dreamers deal implodes

Like the Guardian Angel
watching over the white
children on the bridge.

Jun 12, 2019   How Kamala Harris would provide citizenship
to Dreamers

Jun 13, 2019   Kamala Harris's Plan to Give DREAMers a Pathway…

Jun 24, 2019   Biden says Dreamers should be granted citizenship.

I need an honest YT savior.
I am tired of dreaming.
Tired of praying.

JANUARY 20, 2021

Carlos never liked me touching his things.

"Deja sus cosas alli
se va a enojar!"
My mom would say.

When he noticed it missing,
he chased me around the house,
searching deeply for his red ranger.

Fine, here, don't have a *chiripiorca*

.

- -

Chiripiorca
—Verb—
A series of movements or contractions of the body
experiences when your older brother takes your
things.

       Or a new leader runs your country.

TORTILLAS

I should've bought handmade.

I was desperately looking for
something to accompany my love.

The recipe tells lies.

"You can pair this with *anything*."

I thought it was you + me
                    me + you

We just needed warm tortillas, wrapped,
in your palms. My palms. Together.

So I kept looking.

I kept walking these medium-sized aisles of your
favorite tienda.

The best tortillas are handmade and can only
be bought at Superior Grocers,
down Laurel Canyon, in Pacoima.

Message Read

I picked up *Guerrero* instead.

What's the difference?

                They're
                just tortillas.

FAT GIRLS NEED LOVE

We lay around like wet seals on Danny's bed.

Adriana lays her heavy next to mine
and asks, "So what, David?"
as if I had an ocean of secrets.

Daniela is so quiet at times
she hides her heavy with a pillow or two
I know she has Tinder on her phone.

We talk for hours, and every so often, one of
them cries.

***

We share a yarn we braided using
threes, and made a chain as strong as metal.

"My fat is better than yours," one of them says
or both, I forget.

***

We are from eating just to kick it and eating
just to eat.

We snack on Cheetos and Takis
and hot tea for digestion.

"My fat is stronger than yours," one of them says
or both,
                                    I forget.

3'S

*

The third time he cheated on you, I reaped the confidence from the soil of my heart and told him, "You are my soulmate." "Do you still feel that way?" he asked in return. You can tell he was not in complete shock. He even puffed his chest like a rooster in heat. "If you could do anything right now, what would you like to do?"

Right there, in the corner of ███,

I swallowed him.
All of him.

**

The second time he cheated on you was at ███████ Park. I picked him up in my new car. He reeked of John's Liquor Store—the only liquor store on Van Nuys Blvd and Pacoima that stays open for thirsty men past 2:00 am. He wore short shorts and swollen eyes. We sat on the empty bleachers next to ghosts and nosy trees. I sat one row below him, ready to worship my king. I didn't put him in my mouth that time, but I can tell you every detail and count every vein.

***

The first time he cheated on you with *me* was via FaceTime. It was also the first time we played Truth or Dare, a game we'd entertained for over three years. His desire for attention oozed through his iPhone as he showed me his "new pants"—"They fit you snugly," I replied. He knew what he was doing when he started to undress. He knew I was staring at the outline of his penis. "Your turn," he said. "Cum for me"—

Bust.

I had him more than three times / three others had him before me.

how does it
feel to wonder?

12 | 4

I witnessed you lie to your mother when you married a woman, not a man. They knew you were lying as you stood under him, waiting for her to walk down the aisle of your filth and lies. Your guests passed your secret around like collection baskets get passed around on Sunday church. Like deer in the open meadows, your sin lay in plain sight for him to witness. You fooled yourself if you thought he didn't know about me or the three before. Today was the most challenging day of our imaginary relationship. I still can't decide if people were crying over the horror of mockery of your "vows."

Or out of excitement.

ENSÉÑAME A BAILAR

You leaned in for a kiss—
Right next to the bar at Rocco's WeHo, the only place I was worthy of your lips.
Right next to the strippers and drunks.
Right next to strangers who wouldn't think twice about the ring
       on your finger.

Never tell a Dreamer how much you love them.
Never FaceTime them on their birthday and speak of hypotheticals.
Please don't lie to a Dreamer like *me*.

Because loving you in Spanish was not the same as loving you in English.

It was listening to Jose Jose, Pedro Infante, Bronco, Los Bukis, and Amanda Miguel
on your abuelito's old Panasonic.

I loved you more in Spanish.

The party was loud with music and doubt, so I kept playing our romance
in my head.
Until losing you to the crowd.

Why did you kiss me, *my love?*

All I have left is this poem, a cascade of loss, and $1.63 on my laundry card.

                             My love is better than yours.

MY DACA IS BETTER THAN YOURS

My DACA is better than yours.
My DACA is better than yours.

My DACA is better than yours.

My DACA is better than yours.
My DACA is better than yours.

My DACA is better than yours.

My DACA is better than yours.

My DACA is better than yours.

MY

DACA

IS

BETTER

THAN
YOURS.

TO: USCIS

I am ordering you
to take your time back.

I don't want it.

It wears loose around my wrist.

It wakes me up spontaneously.

It disobeys me at 3:00 a.m.

I wrapped it as a gift.

It looked so pretty in color white with a matching
white bow.

I gifted it to a friend.

He returned my disobedient time.

            ATTN: *Take your curse back*

           I am ordering you
                take
                your
                time
                back.

EVERYONE CARRIES A BACKPACK
For the educators at Nueva Esperanza

Everyone carries a backpack.

Some are blue,
some are pink,
black,
white,
new,
old.

Everyone at the place of learning,
the home of thinkers and dreamers,
on a Monday or Friday morning,

carries a backpack.

On a busy day, when teachers are
teaching, leaders are leading, the staff
is supporting, students are learning,

shoulders start to bruise, it hurts*!*

Agony is inevitable,
                    contracts won't say.

Takes one job, turns to 100.

Doctors,
nurses,
librarians,
encyclopedias,

heroes,
sheroes,
human shields when it comes to that.

It *has* come to that.

Everyone carries a backpack.

FRIENDLY REMINDER

Mr. Dreamer,
I have five years of teaching experience,

and I know everything there is to know about
teaching

trust me when I say that we are ~~never~~ there to
add anxiety while we do classroom
observations

~~pretend~~ we are ~~not~~ there.

I left a note on your desk.

We will follow up with an email on all the
things you need to work on for next time.

Be here by 8:00 a.m. Students are waiting for
you.

We care that you are fully present with
students.

Hello,
I noticed you haven't submitted your lesson
plans this week. Do you need support?

We want to try this new curriculum this year,
and all in favor say "no."

Don't forget your lesson plans are due.

Thank you for doing the work that you're doing.

We noticed you arrived at 7:51 a.m. Is there anything we can do to support you in getting on time?

Coaching session @ 1:30 pm, no calendar conflict. Your prep interrupted.

DATES AND PLACES

Freedom withholds my identity and
places it on a temporary status.

Justice withholds my dreams and places
them on two-year terms
                                                    and dues.

America withholds

                                                                    me.

        What is there left to prove?

NOVEMBER 8, 2016

the day started with hope glistening through the air,

resilience in my heart, pounding its way out

freedom in my pocket, trying to escape

Today,

I am DACA.

Tomorrow,

I don't know.

DAVID QUIROZ, his brother Carlos, and his mother traveled to the United States from Michoacán, Mexico, in 1995. After several years in the United States, he was enrolled in the charter school system known today as Vaughn Next Century Learning Center. He is a product of the afterschool program system, The Boys and Girls Club of San Fernando Valley and later completed his bachelor's degree at California State University, Northridge. As he obtained a bachelor's in English Subject Matter, David began teaching in 2019, pursuing a master's degree in English with an emphasis in creative writing. He has served as a public-school middle school instructor, teaching seventh-grade English at PUC Nueva Esperanza Charter Academy for five years. As an undocumented first-generation American and first-generation college graduate, David was reenergized after each political battle against undocumented people. Upon receiving DACA, David utilized every opportunity afforded to him. *Dreamer Paradise*, his first book, tells the story of one dreamer, as the DACA/immigrant experience is not universal.

WHAT BOOKS PRESS

A N   I M P R I N T   O F

T H E   G L A S S   T A B L E

C O L L E C T I V E

LOS ANGELES

All WHAT BOOKS feature cover art by Los Angeles painter, printmaker, muralist, and theater and performance artist GRONK. A founding member of ASCO, Gronk collaborates with the LA and Santa Fe Operas and the Kronos Quartet. His work is found in the Corcoran, Smithsonian, LACMA, and Riverside Art Museum's Cheech Marin collection.

As a small, independent press, we urge our readers to support independent booksellers. This is easily done on our website by purchasing our books from Bookshop.org.

WHATBOOKSPRESS.COM

2019

Time Crunch
CATHY COLMAN
POEMS

Whole Night Through
L.I. HENLEY
POEMS

Echo Under Story
KATHERINE SILVER
NOVEL

Decoding Sparrows
MARIANO ZARO
POEMS

2018

Interrupted by the Sea
PAUL LIEBER
POEMS

The Headwaters of Nirvana
BILL MOHR
POEMS

2017

*Gary Oldman Is a Building
You Must Walk Through*
FORREST ROTH
NOVEL

Rhombus and Oval
JESSICA SEQUEIRA
STORIES

Imperfect Pastorals
GAIL WRONSKY
POEMS

2016

The Mysterious Islands
A.W. DEANNUNTIS
STORIES

*The "She" Series:
A Venice Correspondence*
HOLADAY MASON
& SARAH MACLAY
POEMS

Mirage Industries
CAROLIE PARKER
POEMS

2015

*The Balloon Containing
the Water Containing the
Narrative Begins Leaking*
RICH IVES
STORIES

*The Shortest Farewells
Are the Best*
CHUCK ROSENTHAL
& GAIL WRONSKY
LITERARY COLLAGE/PROSE POEMS

2014

It Looks Worse Than I Am
LAURIE BLAUNER
POEMS

They Become Her
REBBECCA BROWN
NOVEL

*The Final Death of Rock-and-
Roll
& Other Stories*
A.W. DEANNUNTIS
STORIES

Perfecta
PATTY SEYBURN
POEMS

2013

Brittle Star
ROD VAL MOORE
NOVEL

WHAT
BOOKS
PRESS

LOS ANGELES

Printed in the USA
CPSIA information can be obtained
at www.ICGtesting.com
LVHW040826161024
793856LV00005B/349